AF334823

LESSONS OF RADICAL FINITUDE

Poems by

MICHAEL McIRVIN

PYGMY FOREST PRESS
Albion, California

Previous versions of some of these poems have appeared in the following publications: *The Archer, The Dakotah, Dog River Review, The High Plains Register, Icarus Review, Mobius, The Owen Wister Review, Phase and Cycle, Proscenium, Xib,* . . .

Also by Michael McIrvin:
Love and Myth — Blue Textual Sparrow Press

Supported in part by a grant from the Wyoming Arts Council.

ISBN 944550-29-0

Pygmy Forest Press
Leonard Cirino, Publisher
P.O. Box 591
Albion, CA 95410

For my sons, Jesse and Eli

CONTENTS

I
THE LABYRINTH OF MIRRORS

Lament	3
Drunk and Reeling. . .	4
Blossoms: Melody and Counterpoint	5
In the Fog	7
Your Self Portrait As an Animal	8
Your Eyes. . .	9
In a Dream. . .	10
Someone's Father	11
Believe It	12
Capitalist Gothic	13
Wondering What Could Be About	14
Western Civilization: Fragments for a Libretto	16
An American Fairy Tale	18
The Labyrinth of Mirrors	20

II
ALIEN VOICES

Alien Voices	25
Song of the Drunk	26
Song of the Man-Boy	27
Song for the End of Love	28
Song of Signs	29
Song of the Man Who Sleeps on the Floor	30
Song of Rage	31
Working for the Union Pacific	32
Song for Tom	35
I Met a Man with a Hard Set Jaw. . .	36
Song of the Suicide	37
Old Man's Song	38

III
LESSONS OF RADICAL FINITUDE

Lessons of Radical Finitude: A Fugue in Four Movements   41
Telling Time   44
Cartography   45
Poem for the Woman Who Talks with God   46
I Met the Devil. . .   47
Sketchbook of the Real   49
Loneliness   52
Dream in Two Voices   53
Place   54
You Said, We Have Lost Touch with the Natural. . .   57
Hands   58
Poetry   59
The Muse   60
Amazing Grace   62

I

THE LABYRINTH OF MIRRORS

Lament

Whom will you cry to, heart? More and more lonely,
your path struggles on through incomprehensible
mankind. All the more futile perhaps
for keeping on toward the future,
toward what has been lost. . .
                              Rilke

Mile after mile
over the glistening Earth
the land is folded in white
like crystalline linen,
and milepost after milepost
I mourn the death of love,
its slow agony
through our blood-soaked century,
its final icy gasping
in our own breath. . .

The road winds black
through these hills
like a scar across the pale
shoulders of a woman
who sleeps on her belly,
weeps in dreams of men
in night-colored clothing
binding her, kicking her
with their steel boots,
carrying her away toward
the inevitable future. . .

A distant city's signal fades
and the radio pours only static
into the car, noise sinister
in its mechanical whiteness.
The engine hums, vicious, monotonous.
The tires hum in another key.
It is no longer simple. Symbols
blur, collide, fuse in seamless mass,
and with the push of a button
the agents of apocalypse smile
over the airways, a song of love
on their metal lips

Drunk and Reeling. . .

we skip our voices
over the mirror surface
of Saratoga Lake.
In the gathering dark
we are laughing, borrowing
the songs of curlew and killdeer,
throwing them like wild fast balls
toward the smoldering west.

But when I tire and turn
to speak you are crying.
Ghosts hover here,
you whisper, a father who rants
and dances in the mask of rage,
a husband who was your father,
a mother, frantic and silent. . .

Their ghosts ride on the wings
of the birds whose voices
we have been imitating:
curlew endlessly questioning
as it flees into the night side
of the world, killdeer berating,
swallows mumbling their small songs
as they bounce like stones off the dark
and dissolve to black.

You sob gently into my shoulder
like the dove whose song is mourning.

Blossoms: Melody and Counterpoint

In the unexamined silence
of her proverbial heart
what is real fades
and what is unreal
grows to take its place. . .

In the ditch across the road
from where he sits, sunflowers
turn their faces to the god
in whose image
they are made. . .

Shadows hover in that silence.
Dark and one eyed,
they whisper
in her sleep
that they are beautiful. . .

He watches the plants all day
from the porch, faces yellow
and bearded, at once humble
and radiant, heads
bowed as in prayer. . .

The shadows tell her
she loves their dark blossoms,
and when her eyes open
she does, she breathes for them
in daylight, she is ashamed. . .

The flowers whole beings turn,
like slow dancers with a beloved,
to follow the gently striding sun
as if a slender thread
were strung between them. . .

5

Eventually, she becomes a night—
flower floating on a capricious wind,
brittle petals of guilt and terror
folding always inward
toward what she cannot bear to face.

Thousands of small suns sway,
devout and ecstatic,
in the late August breeze.
He will move closer to listen
for the song they are surely singing.

In the Fog

The white ghost sky
remains empty,
and the horses stand
with brown flanks
to the silence,
heads slightly lowered,
tails slack
like great war ponies
tired of their burdens,
the smell of blood
and unburied flesh.

I whisper your name,
and it joins the implacable
whiteness of the air.
I push the syllables
gently outward with my mind
toward where you sleep
at this early hour,
imagine the notes
entering your ear,
soft, palpable things,
to coax you awake.

The horses do not move
except to shake moisture
from their manes
or snort fog
from dappled nostrils.
Muzzles uplifted,
they listen
to their own heartbeat,
or the movement of air,
or remembered words
of a song for the rising sun. . .

In an hour
you will call,
send the schedule for today,
who will take our sons where,
and nothing more
over copper wire
and into my ear,
talking from the deep sleep
that is your life.

Your Self Portrait As an Animal
For L.S.M.

An antelope-like creature stands
under the waning thumbnail moon,
its hindquarters strong, shapely,
the soft tresses of a sexual tail
flowing from them.

The front quarters are thin, frail,
held to the hind by a ladder of ribs
that show your hunger.
The long feminine neck holds
a feminine head, your thin jaw
curving up to the leaf-shaped ears
of a deer.

Out of the head grow
the heavy antlers of an elk
that betray you.

There are no eyes.

Your Eyes. . .

have always moved through the spectrum of green:
they were the color of deep sea the day we met,
the grey-green of hail clouds when you were angry,
and only a year ago, I swear, they were phosphorescent
as the dance of aspen leaves in early autumn sun. . .

but the range has changed, slipped somehow:
your eyes are the dusty green of used money,
the sullen green of mold and rotting seed,
the green of old linoleum in this house
full of blue-and-black-bodied flies.

In a Dream. . .
for Barbara

I wander east
over the sad Earth
looking for you,
walk through plowed
and moonless fields,
between cows sleeping
in their pastures,
the shallow breath
of newborn calves
flowing about my feet.
I do not find you there,
but in the far ancestral city
that draws you like a drug
in an archway of brick and glass
crying for the first time
in your life, sobbing
into the serpentine brown
shadow of your hair. . .
Your face, you tell me,
aches with all the pain
you have never allowed
yourself to feel.
I touch your chin
that quivers
with the tip of one finger.
Your eyes, large
and angelic, dismiss me
as the tears pull back into them.

Someone's Father

In a barren room,
by the light
of a single lamp,
a man stares
into his open hand,

rolls the blossom
of emptiness
across his palm
and squeezes it tight
into an invisible ball.

He opens his hand,
looks hard again—
through the invisible ball,
the wadded blossom—
at the lines like dead rivers,

squeezes again,
looks, squeezes. . .

Believe It

> *I'll never do this again.*
> *It's a trap. . . A Friend.*

Love will beckon again
across the blue distance,
roll the green marbles
of its eyes, smack
its fire-red lips,
twist the steel springs
of its hips just so,
shake its shining silver
buttocks in the sun. . .

You will try to look away, bury
your face in your one good wing,
endeavor to point your erection
in some innocuous direction,
disguise the regnant beating
of your heart with slush and ice. . .

But, ultimately, you will turn
on the three toes of your one good leg
and walk steadily, ecstatically,
into Love's perfect teeth.

Capitalist Gothic

A millionaire washes his hands
in a pure white sink with gold fixtures
under indirect fluorescent lights.

The curved white of the sink
reminds him of his lover's breasts,
of the smooth curve of his new child's ass.

He looks in the mirror,
into his own laconic green eyes,
dries his hands on a clean white towel,

turns back to the sink
and washes his hands again in water from gold fixtures
by the light, indirect, fluorescent, that does not change.

Wondering What Could Be About

A poem for, and in collaboration
with, Jesse

1

Once there was a boy who wondered
if there was a green city.
He drove the blue streets
in a dented blue Volkswagen
looking for some sign of organic mercy.

Once, he thought he saw his parents
riding together in a limousine,
the great blue boat of connubial bliss. . .

2

He wondered if there were volcanoes
in his world. He looked, not far,
and sure enough there were.

He wondered if there was a Grand Canyon,
a great scar running deep through stone.
He went to check, and sure enough there was.

He watched a little girl on her blue bike
ride through the blue streets, singing.
He watched, jealously, a plane escape

into thin air. . .

He dreamt in color
of dancing goats (green)
of horses (also green)
that move in lines
through the sky.

He dreamt of another goat,
singular (mountain blue),
who smiled as he smiled,
wept as he wept,
who could not dance
for the hole in his heart,

walking away
toward a distant sun,
its horned head bowed.

Western Civilization: Fragments for a Libretto

I

Of Eros and Thanatos

There is this low key dreaming:
the fingers move smooth through ivory teeth
poking holes in the fabric of space
with each and every note.

The maestro plays faster and faster,
nihilisimo, until holes replace the whole
and there is no longer any place to stand
or breathe, just a deep dark where we once stood

surrounded by dark.

II

The Patriarch

A thin legged man with bent erection,
that is really a well-disguised
revolver, and loaded, dances
in the twilight of the world,
dances like a moth, in lonely
erratic circles, driven by the rhythm
of music only he hears. . .

III

Alienation

A man and woman stand far apart,
naked except for their molten shame
that shimmers like satin.
They glance at each other,
sidelong, furtive, with hunger. . .

Each begins to move obliquely
toward the other. Every small
step is a strain. They hold
their arms out like Frankenstein's
monster, as if to embrace,
or to mangle. . .

They move around each other,
a spastic do-si-do, and return
to where they began, hands
now hiding self-induced wounds.
Again each glances sidelong
at the other, as the invisible
birds wheel above them
miraculously.

An American Fairy Tale

Elvis was an angel
whose soul flowed as blue light
from his eyes, rolled mellifluous
as honey from his tongue. . .
a cherub who drank deep
from a celestial cup filled
with proletarian lamentation
that he mixed in his throat
with his own. . .

One day a man in dark suit and tie
gave Elvis a bag of money
to stand in a box, to fold the blue
light of his eyes into its mechanical
light, to let it stream into American
houses and reflect off the passive
faces of the watchers:

So Elvis stands, intermittently, forever,
in a luminous circle with a hunchbacked
electronic father who pats him on the head,
assures him and the watchers,
he is a good boy, in spite
of his angelic ass that moves
like a charmed snake to the music. . .

So Elvis sits forever
in a circle of images, silent
guitar in his lap, lip twisted
into a permanent sneer, eyes
raven-black, without reflection. . .
where he speaks nonsense
and the images laugh, where he
moans parodically, mechanically,
in an affected angel's voice. . .

Years later, it is rumored,
a man who called himself Elvis
in dark glasses and perfect
pompadour, wrapped in the folds
of his own flesh, emptied
a revolver into dancing shapes
on a screen, his face blank
as white noise before the implosion
that sucks even the air
from the room.

The Labyrinth of Mirrors

The room is white, silent.
A man, tied to a chair
in its center, sweats.
Another man in a menacing suit
talks harshly, then
the room is silent again.
He pulls a revolver
from inside his coat,
holds it to the tied man's
skull. His finger moves
and sparks of blood splatter
the clean walls. The tied
man's head snaps sideways,
swings back to center,
his eyes wide, blood trickling
from his mouth. Only *his*
expression changes.
The shooter is stolid,
unmoved. So is the watcher.
The shooter leaves by the red
and white door and drives away
nonchalantly, his gun hand
on the steel-smooth thigh
of a beautiful woman.

*

A firm feminine bottom
moves like a flower in the wind
before the shining red car.
A finger, long, sexual,
runs down its chrome.
The woman, who must certainly
smell of carnations, thinks
the watcher, looks like
the one the shooter drove
away with, but blonde.
The car was the same,
but blue.

*

A black man's face
swims in terror before
the watcher. He is silent.
His eyes are swollen.
His lips bleed. Someone
lowers a tire around him,
sets it on fire. . .

Another image rises
in the watcher's mind:
a face, robes mixing with
the saffron of the flames
flowing in a convective
wind. Eyes, the watcher
remembers, that would not close. . .

*

The shooter holds a can
of beer. He laughs.
The tied man is there
too, eyes blazing,
arms crossed, smiling
unnaturally.

*

Before the watcher's eyes
a flower withers
at the end of a long rope:
its stem snapped, eyes
like over-ripe stamens
popping. . .

The watcher considers
another beer, dreams
of a blood-red sports car
and a woman with hair
like the sun.

The hanging flower sways
in the stiff breeze
like a broken gift
waved in the face
of an inattentive lover.

II

ALIEN VOICES

Alien Voices

I want to sing,
but my voice boils up
out of my intestines
an alien thing,
slams hard against the wind:
the breath pinched to a shriek,
warped to a demonic croaking.
Anguish squeezes out between my teeth.
Fear drips from my bruised tongue.
Children weep.
The birds fly away.

Song of the Drunk

holy the visions . . . holy the abyss!
Allen Ginsberg

This distance bleeds
through me: galaxies,
forests of deep stars
splattered wide across
the black domed universe,
the individual points
of light like furious angels
whose terrible fingers
play music wildly
on instruments of stone
and grief, music of cruel
and complex equations
whose answer is always zero.
I feel it ring every night
in the hollow of my chest.
Not the Blissful-Horn-of-Emptiness,
mind you, not the Womb-of-Things,
but aching, bleeding absence
the vapor of whiskey expands
to fill. I want to howl,
but do not have the courage.

Song of the Man-Boy

I walk through the strange air
thick as blood
remembering a lullaby
from someone else's childhood. . .

the mirror breaks
and now it takes
seven years to mend it. . .

Each footstep slides slow.
Every syllable is drawn out
to its very tail.

The tears roll
so like cold oil
I fear I will be old
years before I'm grown.

Song for the End of Love

Early morning light slants
through the kitchen window,
shines warm, golden on your face
where you sit at the table,
slender chin resting on slender hand,
staring into the back yard
as some face, form, name
that is not mine
moves through you. . .

I sit where I have eaten
my meals for years, shaking
hands folded on the table
just outside the waterfall
of light you bathe in, trapped
in this mental photograph
that will not fade, in the prison
space opposite you where meaning
slips its yoke, where all words
dissolve back to unbroken air. . .

In this recurring nightmare
that could have been designed
by Vermeer, I am condemned to carve
your name into my quick heart
eternally
with my own dead tongue.

Song of Signs

We saw you for the first time,
our two sons and I, in the arms
of another man, pushing
your fine flesh against his
in the parking lot of a bar
under the broad light of day
that fell on us, my sons and me,
like a hammer.

I answered the oldest boy's questions
as best I could as we drove on,
tried to explain a stranger's face,
the language of malediction,
the bone-white of knuckles
against the red steering
wheel of the truck. . .

We stopped, my two sons and I,
by the side of the highway
on our way home to watch three deer
move like light through shoulder-tall
grass: alert, strong, all bucks.

Song of the Man Who
Sleeps on the Floor

The moon rides high and full
through the November sky,
shines on our bed
through window panes
etched with cold,
the sheets turned back,
the quilt, made of the patches
of our lives, folded back too.
In imagination I slide in,
a human knife into its sheath,
and feel clean, crisp cotton
glide smooth over my bare legs,
ass, back, and arms,
sink my head deep
into the feminine roundness
of the pillow, pull the blankets
up tight against the chill.
In a rented room
I lie still in my sleeping bag
and listen to the sound
of no one's breathing
but my own.

Song of Rage

The horse of rage sleeps between my shoulders.
It awakens from time to time, lifts its drowsy head,
its eyes that look through my eyes fierce to behold.
Then it sleeps again. I do not know what its dreams
are made of. The murderer who has never killed
merely sleeps the uneasy sleep of great fire
smoldering. . .

Working for the Union Pacific

1

We sit in the work shack
shivering in early morning dark
waiting for the 55 gallon drum
that is our coal stove
to swallow up the cold,

waiting for the work trains
so we can buckle their iron bellies
shut with rods of steel,

waiting to push the bars into the jack's
orifice that closes the metal doors that release
the rock that lies between the tracks. . .

waiting to use my strong, 18 year old hands,
opening and closing fists to keep fingers warm,
like my partner Julio opens and closes his hands,

horned with arthritis and sixty, waiting
with Julio who curses the weather and his god
for pain in shoulders, knees, loins
in a language I do not understand,

waiting. . .

2

Julio walks with an ache
that runs up and down the length
of his body, that cracks when he bends
like a musical forest in the wind,
an ache so long with him
it is part of his being. . .

Today, he limps and sings in Spanish
as we walk to the end of the spur
where a few work cars sit.
Thirty tons of steel at a time
roll past us gentle as cows to join
the herd at the end of the line.
We are to reconnect the brakes.

I hook up the cars that stand quietly
while Julio waits for the next to arrive.
He rests his gloveless hand on the cold
metal hitch, watches the beast move
toward him through the grey cloud
of his breath. He shrieks as the cars couple,

blood and flesh and pulverized bone
of his ring finger the jism
in their mechanical joining.
He holds his hand up to show me his loss
and two tears fall to the ground,
mix with the red already there.

3

I kneel with the rest of the crew
in the cold belly of a boxcar,
roll the carved knuckle bones
of a man across a broken cardboard
box, bounce them off the wall
shouting *siete*, come *siete*. . .
roll a five and shout
in pidgin Spanish, come *five*. . .
for quarters, for hours.

4

Julio rolls in the ground
fifteen years now, fingerless.
In my dream he dreams of trains
that never arrive on time
or otherwise, his own hell
made of rumors of voluptuous steel.
He crosses himself. He says
God is one eyed and stupid
as any machine. He waits
to be swallowed by the Mother
of Beasts, absent wife who wears
the shattered token of his love
like a jewel in her teeth.

Song for Tom

Drunk on a bus, we are riding
by dead factories in the rain.
Your eyes, small and bloodshot,
glare into the dark at headlights.

I hear you tell your reflection,
part of me bleeds and writhes
in this soil black with the sound
of trains, minuscule part someone loves. . .

Your voice fades into sexless night,
fails you utterly against the turning
dark as you stutter and spit, lower
your chin to your chest and sleep.

In your dreams, as always, there will be
a bell, clapper the tongue of a woman
rain hollow and thunder heavy,
whose ringing never stops.

I Met a Man with a Hard Set Jaw. . .

who told me a tale of woe, of money,
how he worked two miles down
in the Earth's bowels mining coal,
how he pulled the remains of friends
charred and smoking like burnt matches
back to light and air for cash:
Hell nobody else would do it,
and I had a wife, kids, a mortgage.

Everywhere now the air smells of sulphur,
every day the light is too bright
and he works the graveyard
at a chemical plant big as a town,
perhaps doing what no one else will,
the kids, wife, and mortgage gone.
And every morning he drinks whiskey,
watches from his front porch
as light invades from the east
like fire shit into the sky.

Song of the Suicide

Isolate in deep forest,
an inviolate *I* lonely
as all men and women
in the civilized world,
I stare into open hands,
into the frightening
blue text of a revolver.

Trees turn above,
whisper to each other
in hundred-year-old voices
saying . . . what? *dance? dance?*
For one instant I believe
and crouch low to leap
into consummate mortality. . .

But those voices soon drown
in the myriad small voices
that chatter at the same pitch
as my own, and that I long
to send gushing together at once
out a small round door
into the blathering wind.

Old Man's Song

I cough, spit phlegm and blood
into snow, and dream of women
with plush thighs the pale brown
of cheap whiskey, blue eyes clear
as gin, hair floating like a flag
on the blonde wind of desire. . .

In a field of seamless white,
except for the single quarter-sized
spot of flame at my feet
and my tracks leading here,
in the appalling silence grating
at the edges of this song, I watch

the sad white fish of my breath
swim away.

III

LESSONS OF RADICAL FINITUDE

Lessons of Radical Finitude:
A Fugue in Four Movements

*. . . the poet in the time of the world's
night utters the holy . . . In Holderlin's
language, the world's night is the
holy night.*

> Heidegger

1

It is the very old dream
of a woman in her dotage.
She is a lonely, stumbling
blasphemer hurling
half-formed sentences
at the impenetrable wall
of the world's night,
shouting in her delirium
"What must I do?"

Against her will she stands naked
at the center of an endless white
expanse that is the field of time,
and Time, also a being,
bends her over, shoves its bony
white cock between her ancient thighs,
the chaos of time filling her womb,
spreading through her.

Her hair stands on end,
shimmering like phosphorus.
The whites of her eyes
become the whole of her eyes.
She shivers terribly,
ecstatically, trembles awake,
turns on the clock radio
and cries by the vague light
of pulsing green numerals
to country songs about love.

2

This is the sound
of the holy:
an inward breath
followed by an outward:
an exchange of the element
of birds for that of trees:
a beleaguered sigh
enraptured moan
shriek of rage or terror:
the pinched and liquid flow
of this syllabary:
all at some level the same. . .

3

A woman's body and a man's
sink into each other
as they lean against
a black sky that holds
the luxuriant orange moon
of late winter between
its deep and powerful thighs.

"We hold back the final
dazzling apocalypse with sighs,"
she tells him, as the false
stars float like fear above them.
"We try endlessly to fill
our lack with this contrapuntal
breathing."

4

Learn to close your teeth
patiently against the dark,
to lie naked, entwined
in the black, sleek absence
that hums, its tongue always
in your jealous ear.
Learn to suck air
through your dry lips
as the fine blades
of oxygen tear
at your tender flesh.
Learn to plead quietly
with the sky for mercy,
with the silence
for a simple song,
any song. Learn
to love the luminous
and invisible face
that lays like cold air
everywhere
against you.

Telling Time

> *In the company of babies,*
> *one is very close*
> *to the kingdom of death.*
> Galway Kinnell

It is late
and my son's torso,
untouched by sunlight
for months, glows like ivory
by the light of the lamp.

He is liquid
on strong, short legs
as he moves across the room
to search a pile of toys
in the corner.

His belly pushes out
a little way over the edge
of grey sweat pants
like the smallest crescent
of a pale moon,

his rib cage a ladder
of vines that embrace him,
that hold the moon
suspended at the edge
of thin and restful clouds.

I imagine
he is a beautiful clock
of muscle and bone
by which I tell the season,
the hour of the day,

his shoulders slightly
hunched, scapula stuck out
like powerful, white knives
as he prepares to do
that short forward roll

into sleep. . .

Cartography

1

Eli's Painting, Age 21 Months

A long legged purple bird
watches like God from the edge
of the living sea, as a limping
man the color of blood strides
sideways under a hunter's moon,
his head in the clouds,
arms outstretched to embrace
the vastness he moves toward,
ineluctable as rain.

2

Jesse's Painting, Age 3½

A single set of blue footprints
flows out of the rolling sun.
A golden bird flies through green wisps
of smoke, through names written
in the sky, decipherable
only to the initiated,
toward the rune for love that is tucked
in a corner beyond the sunrise
at the threshold to the next room
of imagination, of infinity.

Poem for the Woman Who
Talks with God

For Sharon

As wild and curious as a flower,
the blossom of your face
swaying on its slender stem,
you send laughter through bright
teeth, float it toward me
on a rare wind.

It settles on my shoulders,
around my ears, drifts
into my eyes and down my chest. . .
You cover your mouth,
embarrassed at the beauty
and power of that sound,

the multi-colored charge of heaven
still flowing from your eyes.

I Met the Devil. . .

The body is a great intelligence,
a multiplicity with one sense,
a war and a peace, a herd
and a herdsman. . .
                    Nietzsche

in Coos Bay Oregon
in a run-down motel
that smelled of mold,
of the lumber mills
that surround it,
the bay alive with decay.

He, it, came in a dream,
limbed like any man
but genderless, a patch
of grey where its sex
should be, harsh nipples
on shriveled and empty breasts.

He spoke with a voice
exactly like mine. . .
We have a place for you,
he said. I have come
to take you home. . .
But there is a knock on the door,
a slender voice asking to enter.

My visitor's smoke-grey form
becomes smoke, flows
onto the glass partition
between the bed and bath.
He is etched there staring
over sharp rocks floating in a void.

47

The door never opens
but my ex-wife's dream-body appears
in her flawless blonde skin,
running electric hands
over my chest. We make love
slowly, her thighs pushing
like music against mine,
the room filling with the smell
of earth newly turned. . .

And just as suddenly she is gone.
The devil perches like a raven
on the end of the bed,
his lifeless eyes sad.
Come with me, he says. I tell
him I can't, that I am neither
good nor evil wholly, perhaps both
equally.

He lowers his head abruptly
to his knees, wraps his arms
tightly around them, clasping
long fingers over deep lines
in each elbow, and squeezes.
He grows steadily smaller
until he is the size
of a hovering fly
and with an almost inaudible shriek
disappears.

Sketchbook of the Real

> For Angel, who asked. . .

1

The Artist Posits a Beginning

Nothingness broods on the blank face
of the page, on the great salt sea
where life begins, straddles it
like a lover overwhelmed by hunger,
by no light, no cries of birds,
by no *I* and no *other*. . .

The uninterrupted breath
of nothingness catches, rattles
into rhythm through sea foam
as great heart drum, as seed syllable
of desire, as the fire of Being. . .

2

A raven turns its head
in the rain, looks over its shoulder
and cries. The raindrops fall
like small drumbeats in the trees.
Near here, in the far corner
of the page, a man and woman make love
in a tent to this music, add
their own undulating chorus,
their own synchronous rhythm,
and in their mortal fashion
dream of infinity.

3

A raven, bird of all colors in the palette
mixed, turns its translucent eye
toward the brilliant gaze of the sun.
The eye swallows all the light that falls
upon it, and the light sets the finely
etched brain ablaze. The bird,
in terror and wonder, opens its carrion-
beak to scream the sun's oldest name.

4

A man and woman walk
through the trees holding hands.
They laugh together.
His free hand touches her belly
where their child's veins
are spun in the oceanic dark.

His fingers move over her
shifting roundness, fingers
that will one day point
in brittle silence
to the true center of Earth.

5

Aspen leaves turn in the wind,
the shades of green shifting,
size and shape of shadows undulating. . .
A man turns his hand over slowly,
watches the light move across his knuckles,
and stop, brilliant in his palm
caressing his life line.

6

A woman's finger follows the raven
as it flies through the sun's ocher disk.
Her son's eyes follow the invisible
arc of her pointing, the lift
and sweep of long black wings.

He flaps his arms, runs
in widening circles
through the tall grass
as if to ask, "Will I fly
like a bird when I am older,
Mother?"

7

The Artist Posits an End. . .

before the vast white space
of the page, posits Nothing
as an inversion of the black
center in a raven's eye asleep
on the blank waters of time,
Nothing longing for Something
to displace a portion
of its endless body, of desire. . .

The artist posits Nothing. Dreaming,
he folds the page into a pirate's hat,
covers it with blue and orange flowers
to make a child laugh.

Loneliness

A great blue heron stands
on one leg in shallow water.
Raindrops, the size of coins,
fall across its reflection
as great blue drops rise up
out of the lake, collapse
inward upon themselves.

The bird turns its feminine eye
toward me as rain freezes
my featherless flesh, opens
its mouth like a beckoning lover,
and dances off awkward as a teen-
ager, the harsh cry of love
bursting over rough stones
and water toward the shape-shifting sky
I cannot touch.

Dream in Two Voices

In a sweat-soaked single bed
we dreamt our bodies were silver,
that we flew just above the trees,
rolled like eagles in love
through the air, bright talons
flashing in the sun.

We sailed under the eyes of God
that blinked on and off, neon,
banked sharp off the smooth curve
of God's great cheekbone,
floated with appalling grace
under the bellows of God's nostrils. . .

Love! you shriek over and over
in our single dream. . .
Love! Love! we shriek together
into each other's mouth.
You spread your shining thighs
above the granite thighs of God

and we all shudder, together,
like one being.

Place

1

At the foot of Twin Mountain,
where the first Aspens
meet a certain meadow,
there is a hollow
with grass waist high.
Today I found a photo
of you in its center, smiling,
your hair the same dusty gold
as the grass that stands
brittle and erect, dead
under the long fingers
of autumn sunlight.
You wear a white smock
and faded blue jeans not unlike
those you wore yesterday
when you dropped our sons off.
Several slender bodies
of the plants you stand among
lie cradled in your arms,
rest against your body
like frail children. Your smile
and eyes, like the Mona Lisa's,
belong to no one living.

2

In a dream the grass
of the hollow smolders.
You stand unnaturally erect
among the dead, face gaunt,
frail skin stretched tight
across brittle bone.
The Aspen trees from the photo
lay about like a ruined house.
As I watch, as if through
a window, your neck fails you
utterly, your head falls
to the side, rests
on one shoulder.
You grimace as if crying.
There are no tears.

3

It has been ten years
since I walked into this meadow,
waded through the grass in the hollow
and sat in its center.

The seed heads nod gently
around me, welcome me back.
They whisper secrets together
in the language of grass.

It will snow here soon, they say,
press our bodies to the ground
where we will leave the seed
that will be our children. . .

They say more beyond hearing,
but I know I must bring our boys
to this place where I lay
with their mother years ago.

I will not have to tell them
you walked among these slender beings,
made love as the plants danced over us.
Through generations the grass remembers,

and it whispers. . .

You Said, We Have Lost
Touch with the Natural. . .

Wrist and forearm twist
across the inside of bottle-smooth thigh,
a supple branch extending my fingers
to slide over the small tongue
of your clit, soft bowl edge of cunt,
perfect center of your sphincter. . .
        Nothing moves us to song, you said
Your breath is grabbed, pulled deeper
inside you, voice sucked back
to the low growl of origin,
the ends of your spine pulled
into the arc of a bow
for that arrow of sound. . .
        Religion as experience, you said, is dead
My magician's fingers draw water
from your sacred depths
to spill down your legs onto wildflowers
shaped like hooded monks,
onto stone and grass. . .

Hands

Her hands move
through the slender air
ahead of her voice
shaping syllables,
pushing shy words forward
on their graceful legs,
rolling the brittle hoop
of her laughter
across the Earth.

Poetry

Like a pale flower
that does not know which way to turn
in the last warm days of September
or perhaps the strangely warm days of October
in this the driest of years,

you cock your head this way,
then, slowly, the other, waiting for the muse
to whisper something soft and sensuous into your ear,
or God to say anything in the clean, pure syllables of light,

the late, thick light of autumn.
The neighbor's goose sings down the harsh length of its throat,
a car passes on the highway carrying some perceiver of the world
toward Nebraska at seventy, a brief blip of energy

passing through your field of perception.
You follow it with your eyes,
the ragged blossom of your face
turning on the delicate stalk of your neck. . .

The Muse

She is a southern belle,
righteous, self-possessed,
smelling of sex and magnolias,
wearing amethyst. . .

She is a mad widow
alone in the dark
singing of death
in a minor key. . .

She is called Angel-
Whose-Only-Child-Is-Sound,
she chants in labor
the ecstatic song of making. . .

She is called Eater-
Of-Shit-Heavy-Sickly-Hearts-
Full-Of-Debauched-Words,
like love and freedom. . .

She is Mother-
Of-God-Who-Dances-
In-Syllabic-Light-
Among-Whirling-Wild-Iris. . .

She is a nun
boisterous with silence,
a young girl who shouts
in her dreams. . .

epileptic dancer
with ten-thousand feet,
Mother Goose with a tongue
of stone and steel. . .

She is Manic Bride,
Demon Lover, Mother Wisdom,
Daughter-Of-Folly, Wildly-
Singing-Screaming-Sister. . .

She is the sacrifice
on an altar of innocence,
the altar, the innocence,
the wielder of the knife.

Amazing Grace

> *. . . how sweet the sound*
> *that saved a wretch like me*

> *. . . learn to forget that passionate music. It will end.*
> *True singing is a different breath, about*
> *nothing. A gust inside the god. A wind.*
> Rilke, *Sonnets to Orpheus* (1,3)

For Sharon

In the diamond silence of night,
under the flowering sky,
in the sweet breath of ten-thousand
white galaxies of wild plum blossoms,
I am pissing on the pitch-black Earth
and humming slow and soft to the hymn
you wrap around me like arms
from behind, that you send through me,
the words entering just under
my right scapula, swimming
through my chest and resonating
in my throat like cold creek water,
your words rising like trout
that barely break the surface
before descending back into the deep,
the elemental flowing that is their being.
In this moonless mountain night
your song holds my body like a golden
cocoon, mates with silence within me,
and briefly I am
the absolute joy of breathing
and of death.